HOW CRYSTALS SHINE

True Secrets Revealed

Denecia "Dee" Jones

BALBOA.
PRESS

A DIVISION OF HAY HOUSE

Scriptures taken from King James Version of the Bible

Balboa Press books may be ordered through booksellers or by contacting:

Balboa Press
A Division of Hay House
1663 Liberty Drive
Bloomington, IN 47403
www.balboapress.com
1 (877) 407-4847

Print information available on the last page.

ISBN: 978-1-5043-9419-2 (sc)
ISBN: 978-1-5043-9420-8 (e)

Library of Congress Control Number: 2017919303

Balboa Press rev. date: 01/05/2018

Dedication

I dedicate this book to my family, friends and readers for your courage and support by buying this book. I am grateful for your openness to learn about how crystals help us heal not only ourselves but also heal each other in magical ways.

Acknowledgments

I want to thank those who encouraged me and helped me create this book. Charles Berman, thank you for your guidance and your various contributions to make this book a reality. Michele Townsend, thank you for designing the cover and editing its content. Ann Imberman, thank you for your time and assistance for also editing its content. Brandon Vogts, thank you for creating my beautiful photo on the back cover. Krisana, Thank you for the beautiful photo for the front cover. I want to thank Dr. Lin Morel, my life coach, for planting the seed that prompted me to write this book. Thank you to everyone who I interviewed for the book, without you, there would not be a book. I thank God for giving me the courage and strength to write this book and the gift of bringing these amazing people into my life. My hope is that the content in this book shows readers a new way to shine their light even during their darkest days.

Introduction

Scarcely a day goes by when I don't meet someone who is interested in the strong and ancient powers of crystals.

There are hundreds of books out on the market that deal with crystals. Their authors write in detail about healing elements of crystals and their various mystical properties -- but they forget one important thing: the user's perspective. As a result, the process of learning to use crystals can be intimidating, to say the least, for someone who is new to the subject.

The purpose of this book is to open up the "secret society" of crystal users, and show those who are not aware of this world how sexy, creative and easy the use of crystals can be for millions of people. In order to do that, I want to tell you my own story, and the stories of others whom I have interviewed about how the magic of crystals has touched their lives.

I've included many interviews with people whose lives, like mine, have been touched by the power of crystal. Some of their stories are short, and some are long. Some of these people are renowned experts in the field of crystal healing, and some are average people just like you or me. But the common thread is that all of them have let crystals come into their lives and touch them for the better. I want to let them speak to you as testimonials, so you can read the true stories of people who have felt the light of crystal energy in their own words. You'll see how crystals touch everyone in ways that are common to everyone, and in ways that are unique to each experiencer. But no matter what, they are always powerful.

I hope that you enjoy making a connection to the history of crystals and the people who love to use them just as much as I have enjoyed guiding you on the journey.

"If you want to find the secrets of the Universe, think in terms of energy, frequency and vibration."
Dr. Nikola Tesla, 1942.

Contents

History-Crystals through Time

If you are new to the world of crystals and gems, then you might not know that they are considered among the healing wonders of the world. And in fact, knowledge of the healing powers of crystals is far from new. Crystals have been used for their mystical, beneficial properties since the ancient world. And we don't have to look far to find evidence for that. Crystals are mentioned in the Bible over ten times. And it's clear that the ancient people of Biblical times were aware of the power of crystals and stones.

Just take, for example, how the book of Revelation describes the properties of New Jerusalem, God's heavenly city. New Jerusalem, the Bible says, "shone with the glory of God, and its brilliance was like that of a very precious jewel, like a jasper, clear as crystal. The wall was made of jasper, and the city of pure gold, as pure as glass. The foundations of the city walls were decorated with every kind of precious stone. The first foundation was jasper, the second sapphire, the third chalcedony, the fourth emerald, the fifth sardonyx, the sixth carnelian, the seventh chrysolite, the eighth beryl, the ninth topaz, the tenth chrysoprase, the eleventh jacinth, and the twelfth amethyst."

Clearly, the power of these stones and crystals is held very close to God. Indeed, the book of Exodus described a breastplate worn by a Levitical high priest as containing twelve stones, each engraved with one of the names of the twelve tribes of Israel. "The first row was carnelian, chrysolite and beryl," it said. "The second row was turquoise, lapis lazuli and emerald; the third row was jacinth, agate and amethyst; the fourth row was topaz, onyx and jasper."

Crystals or gemstones have been used throughout history not just by common people, but by kings and queens. Egyptian queens such as Hatshepsut and Cleopatra were historically known to add them to their attire and makeup. In their society, crystals were used by ancient astrologers, diviners and priests, and were revered for their power and beauty. Stones were used in ancient Egypt at least as early as 3000 B.C.E. Amulets and talismans were cut from agate, lapis lazuli, carnelian and turquoise. It has been speculated that the pyramids were capped with crystals to channel cosmic forces into the center of the geometric structures.

The Egyptians pulverized gems and mixed them with liquid to drink as a healing elixir. These remedies were prescribed by matching colors to maladies that ancient patients might suffer. For instance, a jaundiced Egyptian might drink yellow beryl. Bloodstones helped those who were bleeding, and lapis those with blue joints from poor circulation.

But the ancient Egyptian sages also used crystals in

ways more familiar to us. A papyrus from 1600 B.C.E. shows how to use beads of lapis lazuli, malachite, and red jasper for healing. Worn as a necklace, they caused diseases to vanish when they passed through the stones.

But the wisdom of the ancients was not restricted only to Egypt -- and neither was the restorative power of crystal healing. Almost everyone has heard of crystal skulls, but many people think of them as a purely fictional invention, perhaps created for Indiana Jones movies. What you might not realize is that crystal skulls are real artifacts, and that many incredible and even miraculous powers have been attributed to them. Crystal skulls are often beautiful and immaculately-carved objects that many claim originated with the ancient Aztec or Maya civilizations. Some have speculated that the skulls may even have been created with the help of ancient extraterrestrial visitors. If that is true, could it mean that aliens thousands of years ago wanted to gift us with the power of crystal healing? There is certainly something otherworldly about the feeling of well-being that can come from their use.

Whether extraterrestrials deserve the credit or not, it's certainly true that the use of crystals and gemstones for their healing and magical powers spread far and wide across the ancient world.

I want to share with you an excerpt from an article I found about the history of lapidary (the shaping of crystals and gemstones) written by Gerald Wykoff, CSM GG for the International Gem Society:

Gem cutting, or lapidary, most certainly got its start as an offshoot of mundane everyday activities. A stone may have fallen into a fire where the heat caused it to break or flake. Perhaps a sharp edge resulted. Certainly, flint and other hard stones possess sharp edges, but a blade-like cutting edge on a newly flaked piece of rock suggested some very interesting possibilities.

In prehistoric times, man hammered tools from stone, presumably smacking one stone against another. He scratched and chiseled out symbols and primitive writings on hard rock and cave walls – and gradually learned the great secret: some stones are harder than others and therefore they are more capable of inflicting scratches on other less hard stones.

From this very basic understanding, drilling and bruting became possible.

Drilling, one of the first of the lapidary arts, traces its roots back almost 1,000,000 years ago. Primitive peoples learned that rocks could be broken or fractured. The breakage provided random fragments, but ultimately experimentation demonstrated that breakage could also be achieved with some semblance of control.

This same knowledge of relative hardness led to bruting, the shaping of a gem specimen by rubbing one mineral against another harder mineral. The slow and tedious practice of bruting was used for centuries until more refined techniques were introduced.

Given the early date, historians are reluctant to attribute anything quite so intellectual as an understanding of cleavages. It was satisfactory that the breaking, chipping, or flaking of a stone could be disciplined…made to occur in desired directions and depth.

Later perhaps, someone viewed these same stone fragments from a more abstract perspective. They viewed the unusual configuration, texture, or coloring of a piece of stone or mineral crystal, and began to contemplate the possible alterations of a stone for artistic or adornment purposes.

The existence of these ancient artifacts proves how old the art of lapidary is. The artifacts demonstrate that lapidaries had conquered the challenges of sawing, chipping, drilling, polishing and faceting before the time of Christ. The work was rudimentary by today's standards but the principles upon which this work was performed are still with us.

Given this history, it's impossible not to see that crystals have been an integral part of the human experience since the beginning of our history as a species. And crystals and gems could not have lasted so long if they had not been of great benefit to human health and wellness.

In a world that is ever changing, crystals are still a way to heal the energy of billions of people worldwide. If placed in a bra, a purse, a pocket, a car, or a room, crystals can create new energy that heals and is here to stay. In this book, we will talk about how these sexy, sophisticated and powerful gems help us create "the Good Life".

Healing... One Moment Please

I was born into a family that loved good food and good times... all the time. As a result, at a young age I saw most of my family members battle depression, angry outbursts, and other difficult health conditions. By the time I was twenty-one, five of my family members had died of different types of cancer within five years of each other. It was at that point in my life that I realized I was at an important crossroad. I could continue the same life path of my family members who eventually died with poor health due to unhealthy eating, lack of adequate exercise and high stress -- all of the things that I knew led to unhappy outcomes -- or I change my eating habits by taking a nutrition class. That would help me to learn how to eat healthier meals, exercise regularly and properly, and allow myself to be around positive situations to create conditions in my life that align with being happy and healthy.

It didn't take me long to figure out that I needed to choose the latter and that is exactly what I did. Nearly 20 years later, I have no regrets. I look sexier and feel stronger than ever and I link all of my rewards to having the discipline and the love of my body to make those changes.

Basically, I had to give myself authorization to heal my body and reprogram my mind to seek happiness with the foods I ate and the exercise that my body sought, and to align them with the emotional feeling that I felt after all of those experiences.

The first thing that I did was to start reading labels and eat less sugar, less salt and red meat. Most days I would eat more white-meat, low fat meats like turkey, chicken and fish. I also cut my intake of dairy products. I honestly felt that I had an addiction to them! And last but not least, I drank more water and added more leafy green vegetables to each meal. I began to go on an hour-long walk or hike three-to-five times a week. This process wasn't easy in the beginning, but within six months of making these changes, I felt the difference. I had more clarity, more energy to do things that I loved, and my past symptoms of depression and asthma completely disappeared. I finally felt healthier and happier than ever before. And my body looked good in all the right areas.

That allowed me to be open to other changes to come...like dealing with my anger and stress issues. Having been born in the United States of America, I was, of course, a television viewer. But I noticed that television was upsetting me. After watching TV, I would be more stressed out. I felt envy, because I didn't have the new car or the new guy with the new ring, etc.

I decided one day to discard the TV. And from that day forward my life become much more peaceful and purposeful. I am no longer living the way that society thinks I should -- but I am living the way that I feel I should and can. To others, this change made me an instant weirdo. Strangely enough, the one thing I noticed was that even without a TV, I still knew what happened on the news, the popular shows, and in other parts of the world because that was all other people talked about. So, I got to cut the stress and save the expense of a cable TV bill, and instead of watching others live their lives on a TV screen, I created my own life story.

Shortly after this decision, my life blossomed. I met an amazing man with whom I had a great long-distance relationship. He treated me like a queen and I treated him like my king. There was only one problem. Anger and stress started to create distance between us on my part. I asked a friend what to do because I was about to mess up everything that I had created. My life story -- the ultimate TV show -- had poor ratings and was about to get canceled. She gave me great advice. See a therapist for help.

"Great!" I said, "So I live in LA, and like most people in LA, I am now in the secret-yet-cool society of going to see my therapist." Here's the kicker: I saw the therapist for six months and my anger and stress didn't go away. So I asked him what else I could do.

He replied, "Go to a meditation guru."

"Where do I find one?" I asked

"Here is the number for the guy who taught me," he said.

I tracked down the meditation guru, a person named Christian at Green Tree Meditation Center. He conducted small four-day meditation classes. I signed up for them, hoping for more inner peace. Maybe I would even become enlightened and win a Buddha or something. The classes started, and believe me when I say that this guy was the happiest meditation guru that I had ever encountered in my life.

I had never met anyone who was so happy that he just laughed between breaths. Christian scared me a bit because at first I thought that he was joking, but I then concluded he was just jollier than Santa Claus delivering presents on Christmas day. He was the ideal role model for me, and I noticed that he was happy and completely at peace even when challenged -- and that is what I wanted for myself.

During our sessions each day, Christian would teach us the history of Vedic meditation and its various techniques. He connected us with this thing called a mantra which I had never heard of. All of this was exciting and scary at the same time. My ego, the fear, and the anger started disappearing after Christian taught me how to use these tools. After the four days, I felt hopeful and I continued practicing meditation as he instructed me to.

After about six months, I started to notice a difference in myself. My anger started to dissolve. I wasn't as reactive to each and everything that my partner mentioned which I didn't understand or like. I slept and had happy dreams as opposed to the nightmares I previously had about TVs chasing me, or me dying of poor health. I started to have the ability to self-reflect and figure out what my problems were, so that I could adjust and work on resolving the conflicts inside of me and my conflicts with others. All the challenges that I thought I had no control over seemed easier when I meditated and began to receive the answers within me.

Nearly ten years later, I have learned not only the first level of Vedic meditation but also the second level, which deepens my meditation state on a more consistent basis. The decision to let my ego go in order to be more connected to my light, happiness, and inner peace by seeking help and following through on the therapy and meditation changed my life for the better. I knew that it wasn't helpful just for me, but for others as well when my friends began to acknowledge the changes in me. They saw that now I was easier to get along with, and my then-husband decided to also take the meditation class with Christian. I knew that I had made the right decision not only to win that Buddha but to become the Buddha.

First the Buddha,
then the Gems

After my awakening to spirituality through meditation I noticed that deeper emotional issues were coming up for me at a rapid rate. I worked hard to accept inner guidance to resolve these issues. The harder I worked, the more I felt resistance against fully letting them go.

At this point, I mentioned to a friend that I was having difficulty overcoming some deep anger and anxiety. He was a thoughtful person who had worked his way up in the entertainment world and I was anxious to hear what he would suggest.

He said, "Go to a metaphysical store to find something that can help you."

I had no idea what he had just said to me. It was as if he was speaking a whole other language. I had to write down what he said on a piece of paper. I went online to find out what a "metaphysical store" meant. I wanted to make sure it wasn't, something dangerous. Once I found it wasn't I was on my way to buy myself something special.

The store was a small shop that had a selection of colored rocks in containers tagged with their names. There were works of art, and all kinds of items I had never seen before. This was the beginning of a new world for me. Although it was a new experience, something about it felt like déjà vu. I felt comfortable and drawn to exploring it. I clearly looked nervous and confused as I browsed around, obviously not knowing what I was looking at, and a young man came up to me and asked, "Can I help you find something?"

Nervously, I prayed that I could come up with an answer that sounded correct. I replied, "I have some problems, and a friend of mine said I could get help with them here. But I don't know where to start."

He asked, "What are your issues?"

"Anger and anxiety," I whispered.

"I know exactly what you mean. Most people come in here with the same issues. Let's go over to this area, I have a crystal that can help you," he replied.

"Crystal?" I thought. "I've never heard of that before. Sounds cool."

As we walked to them, I was mystified by all the different types of these beautiful items that I'd never seen before. I hoped he would explain how they could help me and how I should use them.

"Rose quartz," he indicated. "It helps resolve anger and anxiety. Put it in your bra and under your pillow at night. It should do the trick."

"How does it do it?" I asked.

"Well, let me look it up for you. Here you go. Read this to get more in-depth information," he said, handing me a book.

"OK, I said.

The first line of the description of what a rose quartz

is let me know that this was the crystal that I was meant to seek: "rose quartz is the stone of unconditional love and infinite peace."

It was at that point that I realized that anger cannot exist at the same time as unconditional love. I immediately grabbed the beautiful pink crystal, kissed it, and bought it. When I left the store, I added it to my bra cup over my heart. I felt uncomfortable for a little bit, but after a short while I no longer felt it. It was as if the crystal had become a part of me. I slept with my rose quartz the first night, and I fell in love with it. The crystal brought me more inner peace. My deep anger changed to inner peace -- just as I had hoped it would when I walked into that mysterious store ready for a new experience.

Rose quartz was also an ideal gift for my friends who shared the same symptoms. I didn't tell them what it was. I just told them to wear it in a pocket, or a bra and sleep with it. Each and every person thanked me for their gift. They said it helped them feel happier, get more sleep and have more clarity about their anger and anxiety. They asked me where they could buy more.

That is when I knew that these crystals were not just mind over matter. They were miracle workers repairing the parts of us that we sought to connect with peace and power. I then shared my story with my friends. Each of them was very happy to discover this gift that had been previously unknown to them.

When I gave them this treasure, they were desperate to get help, and I was there to help them connect with the healer. In this case that healer was rose quartz. If I had told them my story first, they probably would not have

15

been open to this unknown item. They may even have thought the good result was just my imagination.

Since that day, I have given away hundreds of crystals to close friends and family members -- and these crystals have really helped them get through some major challenges. Instead of hiding the fact that these crystals are healing the energy inside and outside of us, I have been guided to write this book about crystals and bring the darkness of these beautiful gems into the light so everyone can use them to live a better life. Rose quartz was the first crystal that I purchased -- and it won't be the last.

Celebrities

Even if you have heard of crystal healing before, you might be surprised that many famous people also use crystals for healing and enlightenment. In many ways, celebrities hold a mirror up to us all by letting us compare the way we conduct ourselves to the way they do. We don't all have the same friends or family members that we can compare notes about, but we all know about the same celebrities. Many of those people whom we admire could perhaps get a lot of their creative energies from crystals! Let me give you some examples of well-known users of crystals.

Adelle

The legendary singer says crystals have helped her with her stage fright. According to *The Sun*, she said, "I was so nervous about my comeback show and I was panicking. I was out of practice and I was busy being a mum. But it was one of the best shows I've ever done and I had these bloody crystals in my hand."

But she lost her crystals before the Grammys, where technical issues plagued her performance.

"Then the Grammys came and I lost my f**king

crystals!" she explained. "I had a gig two or three days before them and I think I left them at this venue.

"It turned out to be the worst, most disastrous performance that I have ever done. Well, apart from one really early on when I was doing a gig in Angel and I got so drunk I fell off my chair. But I got some new crystals now and everything's been going well."

Describing herself as a "hippie," Adele added that she now meditates before concerts so that she's "in the zone."

"I mean literally I'm turning into a walking cliché but I'm proud of it—if it means my shows are good then I don't mind," she said. Adelle seems to love her crystals.

Katy Perry

The singer apparently learned about crystal healing from Madonna, who Perry says gave her the number of a crystal healer after the singer's public breakup with musician John Mayer in 2014.

"I don't stay single for long," Perry told *Cosmopolitan*. "I carry a lot of rose quartz, which attracts the male. Maybe I need to calm it down with the amethyst."

Kylie Jenner

A couple of months ago, the social media star (aka King Kylie) shared an image of massive crystals larger than both of her feet, acquiring over 794,000 likes.

From the regular gal who lives next door, to a major celebrity, crystals are the new hip way to get the energy that you need to get better results. Crystals are taking our society by storm and they aren't letting go!

David and Victoria Beckham

The internationally famous soccer great and his wife, formerly known as Posh Spice, have both become enamored of the power than can be found in crystals!

David: "We've both been into crystals since moving to L.A." —*Daily Star*, December 2010

Victoria: "I'm a very spiritual person. I travel with my crystals. I've got all different colors. It's just something that I'm into. I am quite a superstitious person. I don't walk under a ladder. If I see a magpie, I salute." —*Allure*, March 2011

Heidi and Spencer Pratt

"Speidi" are another famous power couple that has discovered what crystals can do. The two, who are famous from the TV series *The Hill*, both use crystals and have some amazing stories about them.

Heidi: "I was not in the right mind frame to make that decision [for plastic surgery]. I was in so much pain. I was literally crying every day…I felt the crystals were helping. Whether it was just metaphorically, or just a placebo effect, [they helped]. Spencer was like, 'Wow! These crystals are really working' too. We were just not at a good place at the end of *The Hills*." —*Vice*, February 2016

Spencer: "I am so addicted to crystals, it's like a sickness. I've spent $500,000 on crystals this year. I checked my bank account last night, and I have $203 left…[On Valentine's Day] we hung out with our puppies and cuddled with our crystal. It's supposed to bring love. There's a whole science to this — I'm not crazy." —*Life and Style*, February 2010

Kate Hudson

Kate has been one of the most successful actresses in Hollywood through the 2000s and 2010s. And if you went into her home, what would you find on her bedside table? According to her in a 2013 interview, it's "A crystal bowl filled with rose-quartz heart crystals that my mom gave me for Mother's Day one year."

Miranda Kerr

Miranda is currently on top of the world as one of the planet's most popular and successful models. And she certainly deserves her place on this list. She is a huge user of crystals:

"You may have read in some press articles that when I'm asked what's in my handbag...I often mention a crystal wand or a Rose Quartz crystal. My crystal wand is incredibly special to me, and is one of my most cherished items. It's made of Clear Quartz and is studded with Rose Quartz. Clear Quartz is a great stone for gathering, directing and transmitting energy...it can also transform negative energy into positive energy, and Rose Quartz is a wonderful stone to heal and protect the heart, balance emotions, release stress and tension, and encourage love and self-esteem. Crystals can be used in many different methods of healing. In addition to using on a specific area of the body, or on Chakra points to locate blockages to cleanse and heal them, they can also be used in massage. Massaging the body with a crystal helps to release tension from the body, while at the same time the stone's healing energy is transferred to the body. I hold my crystal during meditation, prayer, deep belly breathing, and use it to

infuse my Luxurious Rosehip Body Oil with positive vibrations prior to a massage. I also sleep with it nearby so I'm constantly receiving its special healing energies."
—KORA Organics, February 2015

Bethany Cosentino

Bethany is a celebrity from the world of music -- she's the creator of the rock duo Best Coast, for which she sings vocals, and also plays guitar and piano. "I hate flying," she once confessed, "so I'll be on a plane and I'll be that weirdo in the corner with these in my hand. One is for anxiety and depression, one is Moonstone which helps with clarity, this other one. They're basically all to help center and balance you." —Vice, July 2015

Crystal Renn

This amazingly successful model has also written a book about her experiences. She is not unaware that with a name like crystal, it would be hard to avoid learning about how transformative crystals can be! She said, "I've been collecting crystals for many, many years for healing purposes and decoration...I guess since my name is Crystal, I have no choice." —*Harper's Bazaar*, January 2016

Shirley MacLaine

Shirley is an Academy Award- and Golden Globe-winning actress with an incredible, legendary career. And she has been speaking loudly about the power of crystals for many years. Here's what she wrote back in 1989: "The first time someone gave me a natural quartz crystal I laid it in the palm of my hand to examine it. I was fascinated. Not only was it beautiful: it seemed to have dimensions within dimensions, reflections within reflections. I held it up to the sun and allowed myself to sort of go inside it…In a darkened room I placed the crystal given to me at eye level on a high table. Then I lit a candle behind it and sat down next to it. I gazed into the crystal and projected positive and loving thought forms into it. I had the feeling that they reverberated back to me. It was very pleasant. Then I tried negative and angry thought forms. I had the feeling that that is what I got back. I became uncomfortable. I made my choice. For an hour I sat in front of my crystal with the candle behind it and just gazed into it with thoughts that were as pleasant as I could conjure up. It was a wonderful evening. And I slept better than I had in weeks." —*Going Within*, 1989

These celebrity testimonials clearly demonstrate how powerful crystals can be in a person's life. But it's not just famous people who can receive these benefits. Crystals are truly for everyone -- man or woman. I want to give you both a female and a male perspective on the crystal experience before we move onto testimonials from crystal entrepreneurs and average users.

The Female Perspective

I always think it's good to get both a female and male perspective on things. And who better than me to give the female perspective on crystals? Since I've connected to crystals, my life has changed immeasurably for the best. I could say "better," but crystals are really the final step on personal journey to healing that has had many stages.

Practicing yoga was my first method of healing. It helped me to breathe deeply -- and to be open and flexible to many things. Meditation was my second method of consciousness. It helped me to be open to new ways of thinking, being, and receiving guidance. And last but not least, crystal energy is my third love. Crystals allowed me to add their energy to mine, and to heal my own in countless ways.

Whatever I was lacking, crystal energy was the beautiful heaven-sent bandage that made my pain and suffering in that area get better. My decision to use crystals led not only to my own healing. In fact, most of my friends have received unsolicited crystal as gifts to heal their challenges. And I can describe my experiences with crystals as nothing but an amazing journey of adventure.

To this day, I still have positive results with crystals, as do those friends who didn't even know what I had given them until I mentioned that they were crystals -- crystals that could help them heal their challenges. My favorite method of usage is still to place my crystals in my bra. Just for that reason, I made a bra that has custom pockets in it so that my crystals don't fall out.

The decision to create a bra with a crystal pocket came from one of the experiences that also brought me to writing this book. A few years ago I was at a business networking event in San Francisco. I was standing in a high-end restaurant in a circle of people when I decided to change my high heels to the comfortable flats that were in my purse. When no one was looking, I stepped out of the circle and bent over to grab my shoes. As I did so I felt the sizeable heart-shaped rose quartz crystal that I had placed in my bra began to fall out. I watched in horror while it slid across the carpeted floor in the middle of this circle of people that I had just met minutes earlier. So there I was, looking at everyone staring at my rose quartz -- and some extra shoes that I had just dropped on the floor in my fear. Soon enough, they were also staring at the grin that was on my face because of the hilarious looks of fear and confusion that I had seen.

In that brief moment, I decided to just pretend that I didn't know what happened, and that the shoes and the crystal were not mine. Then reality sunk in and my love for my crystal (more than for my spare shoes!) made me realize that I shouldn't give it up. I knew that I needed to provide an explanation of what the heck had just happened. It was as if an alien had dropped a nuclear bomb on the floor and no one had time to react. I had no other choice but to smile, pretend it wasn't an accident, and bend over to pick both items up. Then I needed to explain. I slowly bent over, switched my shoes, and grabbed my crystal.

"What is that?" someone asked me.

"Oh, this?" I replied. "This is a rose quartz crystal. It must have fallen out of my pocket."

"You don't have pockets," the person astutely pointed out.

"Oh, you're right! I meant my purse," I explained, hoping that they didn't see it fall out of my bra and call me on it. "As I was saying, this is a rose quartz crystal. It allows the user to open their heart to love, and to reduce anxiety and anger. I have had this one for many years and it is very beneficial to me. It has helped me feel more inner peace. I enjoy having it with me because it really has helped me."

After a few moments of silence, I started laughing because I was so nervous, and I could tell they felt the same way. Thankfully they began to laugh too. "You are funny. I have to say I have never had a conversation like that -- where I hear something drop on the floor, and see that it's not only heart shaped but pink, and that there is an extra pair of shoes out of nowhere along with it!" the gentleman replied.

Laughter, laughter, laughter. Thank God for the gift of laughter!

"Well, that was a surprise to me too!" I admitted.

"I think this is so funny," the man told me. "Your new name with me is 'Crystal Gal.'"

"Sounds good to me!" I replied with nervous laughter.

In the end, the people who had no interest in talking about crystals left the circle. The people who understood or wanted to understand more of what had just happened, stayed. One guy asked me, "How do you use crystals and why?"

"Well," I told him, "before I used my rose quartz I had a lot of anger inside. My rose quartz is the only natural healing method that has helped me resolve it."

"Hmm. You know, I am having a difficult time with my teenage daughter and her anger right now," he replied. "Where can I buy one? And how should I present it to her so that she doesn't just reject it?"

"Well," I explained, "you can buy it at any metaphysical store that sells natural crystals. It sounds like she could use a rose quartz crystal too. You can give it to her as a necklace. Or a heart shaped rose quartz would be nice touch. Mention to her that she can wear it and have it under her pillow to sleep well."

"Thank you," he said, "I'll let you know how things go." And he left.

A few months later, I saw him at a networking event and he immediately came up to me. "Hello! How are you?" he said.

"Hello!" I replied. "How did things go with your daughter? Did you buy the crystal?"

"Yes, I did!" he exclaimed. "Thank God! It really was a life-changer for us. The nasty fights that she used to have with us are now healthy conversations. She even comes up to hug me now. She is like a new person and she loves -- absolutely adores -- her heart-shaped crystal. She takes it everywhere with her. At school, she has it in her backpack. I think she puts it in her purse or pocket too. Thank you so much for suggesting it."

At that point, I was stupendously happy that I had dropped my crystal on the floor, and that the accident had led to helping him create peace inside his daughter and in his home. I began to actually like my new nickname, Crystal Gal. Being the Crystal Gal wasn't as bad as I thought. It makes the child in me feel like a superhero -- one who is connected to other kickass Crystal Gals healing the human race with our crystals.

People ask me all the time what things I have done with my crystals. Well, I have put them in my bra, in my purse, inside my wallet, and under my pillow. I have worn crystal jewelry and drank water with crystals in the glass.

Most recently, during my birthday weekend, I bought a Chakrub crystal sex toy, the Rabbit Jade, also known as the White Jasper. I had never owned such a precious gift. I felt that using it allowed me to have a deeper, meditative connection during the sexual experience than I had ever known possible. I highly recommend buying one or more Chakrub quality products. You won't be disappointed.

Elicia Magaña, - Crystals and the Businessperson

My next interview was a quick stop in with Elicia Magaña, a business owner of KIMA Event Management & Consulting, an event planning company. She told me she discovered the power of crystals on a vacation in Sedona.

Elicia said she uses crystals regularly. Her most recent purchase was three bracelets - hematite, fluorite and quartz. She doesn't even have to wear them daily for them to calm her mind and encourage discipline and good habits. And she advised everyone to try looking for crystals. "Go to a crystal shop! Browse and ask questions. There are so many ways to carry them - ring, necklace, bracelet, in your purse...The list is endless!"

"I bought a necklace to attract love right before I left Sedona, AZ," she remembered. "When I got to the airport, I noticed the necklace wasn't on my neck any longer. Maybe it had fallen off. But looking back on that time, December 2014, it was when my relationship was broken and it was time for me to let go. I didn't until three years later, but I took it as a sign that it wasn't the time for love." That's part of the magic of crystals -- sometimes they send you messages in ways that nobody could ever expect or predict.

"I would love for people to explore and use crystals as a bonus to whatever actions or treatments that they are already doing to heal or grow!" Elicia told me. "Crystals are fun, interesting, beautiful and beneficial."

Elicia's crystal story is short so far, but it is still very important. Why? Because it shows that small crystals can make changes in the life of anyone. And you don't have to be an expert or crystal guru to take advantage of the great powers that they have!

Male Perspective

Dane Flanigan -Crystals and Business/Personal Growth

To get a male perspective on crystal healing, I decided to speak with Dane Flanigan. Dane is a serial entrepreneur who is originally from Ohio, but has lived in LA for almost 20 years. He loves it here in California -- especially the weather. "Weather can be very important to mental wellness, which can be harder to achieve when it's about sixty degrees and raining in May, the way it often is in Ohio!" He says.

Dane has been happily married for three years, and is doing very well as a consultant, running a business that assists other businesses with his services. Dane uses his expertise to help companies improve their strategy to grow their sales in their particular industries. "I look at their books, look at their company numbers and ways to maximize their profits within their industry." And he has started a few businesses, from a restaurant to real estate, including a trendy bar in downtown Los Angeles on 2nd and Hill called Ebanos Crossing.

Clearly, Dane has a very diverse background in

working with different types of business structures. Though he is, young, he is very wise, which means he is not all business -- he is also attuned to the power of crystals.

Dane told me that he first heard about crystals through his experience going to Yoga classes. Around the same time, he also started learning about chakras, and he realized the world of energy was made up of chakras and crystals. This, he told me, allowed him to see the reflection of energy and how one can channel it not only to help oneself, but to also help others.

I asked Dane what brought him to explore Yoga initially. He told me, "Physically I was looking for something that would allow my body to go through that spiritual path that allowed me to stretch and push myself into positions. Then there came the mental benefits of it. The hardest thing for me in Yoga wasn't the physical exercise -- it was the mental exercise. The meditations. The breath work. Yoga is a series of steps, but the main exercise is really focusing on the breath. And at that time for me, breath work was really difficult to do."

Breath work can be difficult for anyone. But Dane's is an inspirational story because he has been an experienced Yogi for four years now!

Still, Dane told me, "I'm learning every day. I am just learning how to clear my mind. In the past that was really difficult for me. My mind is constantly thinking -- which isn't good. With Yoga and Meditation, I have been able to slow my mind down and it is actually helping me with clarity with my thoughts."

Dane taught me about Nikola Tesla, a famous inventor

from the past who was a serial entrepreneur as well. Tesla invented the current that we find in batteries today. He also invented shortwave radio, which is technology used in today's cell phones. But the reason Tesla decided to become an inventor was that he wanted to discover a way to reach out to his dead mother. Tesla believed that energy was an eternal current, and if you reversed some of that current you could reach out and touch different frequencies. Just like the old Bell Systems slogan: "Reach out and touch someone."

Knowing Dane had the wisdom that he did, I wanted to know how he became familiar with crystals for the first time. "Well," he told me, "a friend of mine gave me my first crystal as a gift. The crystal allowed me to visualize the energy. I believe energy is effervescent and it's everywhere, and crystals help you channel that energy. Like on a dial, they help you tune in a bit."

This was exciting! And naturally, I wanted to know more. I asked if that particular crystal he'd received had worked -- did it help him find what he was seeking? "I had just come from a project that I left," Dane told me. "At that project I lost my temper and yelled at someone. I think when you are doing so many things, you're in a rush, and you have a lot of pressure upon you, you have a tendency to treat the task as more important than you do the journey. You are looking so far ahead that you forget about how many steps there are and how many people there are along the way. I actually had never yelled at anyone before that point and I felt very bad about it. I left the project because of that incident, as well as the pressure that was on me because of it. The crystal that my friend had given me was able to allow me to communicate with people better. I believe that is what I needed to do, instead of focusing on the many things that I needed to do I needed to focus on improving my communication with others who could help me get things done along the way."

But Dane's crystal story did not end there. Rather, crystals have continued to help him immensely in his daily life. "It took a while to get used to figuring what the crystal was for," he admitted to me. "I had to really focus in on what it was and why people love it so much. I found that it helped me engage with myself to figure out where I needed to be. If you are able to meditate with crystals, that is something I think beginners should consider. It helped me very much."

Crystals may be inorganic, but for Dane, the most important thing about them is still the human connection. "The coolest thing for me," he explained, "Is when I go out and see a store with crystals and can be surrounded by not only all of the energy of the crystals but by that of the person who is there with me. That person is showing you the crystals and telling you about the crystals and what the crystals mean to them. They also talk about where they found them, why they are here, why they sell the crystals and where they mined them, all of which is fascinating. Every person who owns one of these stores has a story to tell about how they got into the business, where they found the crystals, and what the crystals mean to them. That information will have an effect on why you like or dislike the store or person. I may not like that person because they don't seem to really care about the crystals or the clients, or they may buy their crystals from a cheap quality vendor."

In short, crystals have changed Dane's life immeasurably for the better, and they aren't incongruous at all, even in his usually serious world of business and investment. Dane is living proof that a masculine energy can benefit hugely from crystal power. Looking at the history of crystals, there is so much information that has benefited us all for a very long time, and that's true for men and women alike.

Joseph - Beads of Paradise NYC

To find out more about the way that average consumers might find and encounter healing minerals, I spoke to Joseph, from the company Beads of Paradise in New York City, for my first interview of the book. Joseph has been with Beads of Paradise about eight years, serving as the executive manager for the last seven. His company serves hundreds of clients each day, the vast majority of which are local/US-based, but with quite a hearty helping of folks all around the world. Joseph and his company have shipped items to every continent on the globe at this point, except Antarctica.

One of the things I found interesting about Beads of Paradise is that they have a different M.O. than most bead stores, rooted in their origins. The company started as a small African art gallery, located in New York's East Village in the late 1980s. During the '90s, their travels expanded to include Asia and the Americas, and they shifted their focus to include more beads, wearable jewelry, textiles, and unique goods from all over the world, at a variety of price points to meet customers' needs. Along with that came the move into their current location in the historic Flatiron District in NYC.

Beads of Paradise offers a vast selection of products, from contemporary Czech seed beads and jewelry-making components and findings, to unique and antique art from all over the world. In addition, they carry a carefully curated range of high-end, semi-precious stone beads, teach introductory beading courses to beginners, and have an in-house repair service for beaded jewelry. They also carry unique clothing, home and personal accessories and their own handmade line of modern jewelry, prayer beads and imported ethnographic jewelry.

According to Joseph, the store simply aims to have something for everyone. The owner dreamed big, and imagined an exotic bazaar similar to ones he had seen in his travels, placed right in the heart of New York, with items from all over the world, and exceptional customer service - a place where it is an experience merely to walk into the store. And that is certainly what they have created.

I asked Joseph what patterns he had seen over the years in his clients' natural stone bead purchases, and what he told me confirmed my instincts about the popularity of mineral healing in today's culture. "For a little while, he said, "many of the trade beads from Africa and Asia were not quite as popular as they had been, and we have seen more emphasis on semi-precious stones and contemporary styling. However, I think we are seeing a new demographic of customer, in addition to our loyal following we have had for years. This new person may be slightly younger, but they are independent in thought and style, and looking for something more substantial, more authentic than merely purchasing an off-the rack item from a fashion chain that comes cheaply made from overseas by the container-full. They want a piece that has history, that can be customized just the way they want it, that resounds with them on a profound level." Crystals are sexy, and the young generation of customers coming into Beads of Paradise knows it!

Beads of Paradise spends a tremendous amount of time sourcing the stones that they sell, and aims to have the most exquisite in quality and uniqueness. They carry a lot of stones that others do not, ranging from rare Ethiopian black opals and authentic quahog (wampum) beads, as well as fine Tibetan quartz and talismanic agates from the Silk Road region, known as Suleiman or Solomon's Agates. They have been honored to source hard-to-find antique beads for museums and academic institutions. For many of their clients, just a small token or wearable piece of a certain stone is desired for its metaphysical properties. They love that they can come in and design a custom piece that they make for them, rather than ordering something that may not be the right size, or style, or may even be of questionable materials and workmanship.

I asked Joseph if there was anything fun that he was working on at the moment and that he wanted me to let my readers know. He told me, "We are insanely busy with projects right now. Many of them will have to stay under wraps for the moment, such as the ongoing projects we have in collaboration with some big name fashion companies, and a very prestigious cultural institution for whom we are creating reproductions of important historical jewelry. But I'll let slip about a couple things.

We're pushing forward on our website very diligently, trying to bring the experience of being in the store to a broader audience of people who can't make it physically here for one reason or another. Part of that is our upcoming Yogi Project, where we are partnering with teachers from our local yoga community to launch a line of jewelry and custom prayer beads inspired by the individual teachers' practices."

But most importantly, of course, I wanted to know from Joseph how he thought his business could change the world. His answer was an inspiring one: "We simply try to do what we can, where we are, with what we have. We are at an odd point in history I think, where so many people have so much in comparison to most of the history of our species, and yet, our modern societies aren't always the best at providing nourishment and growth for the human spirit, or getting any of our resources to other global communities who are in need of them. I humbly like to think that we can continue the path we are on, bringing a little bit of beauty and exposure to the aesthetic richness of other cultures to people in NYC and beyond, working with artisans and communities overseas as directly as possible, while supporting our little family of staff. That would be a win as far as I'm concerned."

Stories from the Soul

Nicole Mixdorf - Crystals and Yoga

Along with crystals, many people around the world today are discovering the great power that can be accessed through the ancient Indian practice of Yoga. To find out more about how Yogic meditation and crystals intersect, I got in touch with Nicole Mixdorf, a corporate wellness consultant, and the owner of a national wellness company called Balance by Nature. She wrote her crystal story for me, and I wanted to share her inspiring background with you in her own words:

I spend my days inspiring people to create a more balanced lifestyle. I started my own business five years ago, after experiencing the debilitating health effects of a stressful work environment in the fast-paced corporate world. I successfully worked my way up the corporate ladder to be an executive director at a global firm, only to have my whole life affected by a stress-induced health condition. I discovered how difficult it is to give 100% of yourself to anything when you don't feel well. When the health condition started impacting my ability to successfully do my job, I knew it was time for a break to heal my body. It was during this time that I discovered the healing power of crystals.

I went down to Deepak Chopra's center in Carlsbad, California to attend a healing retreat. My experience there completely changed my life in the most profound ways. I was at a crossroad in my life when I arrived, not knowing what direction my life should take. All I knew was that my successful corporate career was slowly killing me, leaving me physically and mentally drained. I had always had an idea to start some type of Yoga business, but the idea of throwing my income and security to the wind terrified me. It didn't even seem like a real possibility. All of that changed at the retreat.

On the first day I went into the gift shop where I found a beautiful stone that called out to me. It was round and smooth and fit into the palm of my hand perfectly, with gorgeous iridescent streaks of light blue and green. It was kyanite with fuchsite. I didn't know at the time what properties this stone carried, but it felt good in my hand, so I took it with me to all of the sessions.

In one of the most powerful sessions, Deepak Chopra shared with us the three most important questions you should ask yourself every day. He says that you should ideally ask these questions right before you meditate. Sit comfortably, close your eyes, take a few deep breaths in and out of the nose, and then ask yourself the following questions: 1) Who am I? Not this is my name and this is what I do, but who am I REALLY, deep down inside, on a soul level? 2) What do I want? If I could have anything and be totally fulfilled, what do I want? It could be for now, or what I want in my future. It's so simple, yet we never think to ask ourselves this powerful question. 3) What is my purpose? How can I give? How can I serve? Deepak says that we all have special gifts to share with the world, and that our purpose is highly intertwined with these gifts. What are you truly passionate about? What do you love to do so much that you lose track of time when you're doing it? What do you love so much that you'd be willing to give it away for free because you love doing it so much? He says that if you can find a way to use your special gifts to help others, then that's what your purpose is. So ask the questions every day, with a real intention of wanting to know the answers. And then let the questions go. Take a few more breaths and begin your meditation. The answers will start to flow in a matter of weeks, in moments of inspiration, in conversations where someone says something that resonates with you, or in signs that appear to guide your path. Once you start receiving the answers, you continue asking the questions. You simply start reaffirming the answers after asking. Using my little kyanite/fuchsite crystal, I discovered just how powerful these questions are.

One evening back in my hotel room, I held my crystal in my hand as I started asking these questions, embarking on a powerful meditative experience. I was trying to heal my body from painful ulcers and a thyroid condition. I was trying to find direction. What I received was the most incredible gift from within. I got inspired to systematically place the crystal on all of my chakras, starting from my root chakra and going all the way up to my crown chakra. At each of them, I held the crystal and started saying "This is not who I am. This disease is not who I am. This imbalanced life is not who I am. This is NOT WHO I AM." I repeated it, as I slowly went up each of my chakras. When I got to my heart chakra, the most profound thing happened. I circled that crystal around my heart and cried "THIS IS NOT WHO I AM!" and in that instant, a deep, penetrating green energy poured straight from my heart with a sudden and instant knowing of who I am. I was completely connected to the light within my heart where the whole universe resides. It was divine love, and it felt like home. In that moment, I knew who I was…I was a spark of the divine. I lived in the realm of infinite possibilities. For the first time in my life, I truly knew who I was, and it was beautiful.

Over the course of the following weeks, I meditated with that crystal every day, continuing to ask the three most important questions. The answers flowed to me as if I was a magnet drawing them straight into my heart. I quickly discovered who I am, what I wanted, and what my purpose is. I wanted to start a corporate wellness business where I could take these healing practices into stressed-out work environments to teach other busy professionals how to find balance and lead healthier, happier lives. Starting my business was my destiny. My purpose is to inspire others to create powerful changes in their lives and raise the collective vibration. This beautiful crystal helped to guide me toward these truths.

I soon discovered a little crystal store near my house that had a wide variety of beautiful crystals. I would go in and see which crystals stood out to me. Then I would read about their healing properties. In order to choose the right one, I would hold them in my hand, close my eyes, and see which one felt the best. I started using different crystals when I would meditate, depending on what my intentions were and what I was trying to achieve. I found an amazing book called <u>The Crystal Bible – A Definitive Guide to Crystals</u> by Judy Hall. I highly recommend this book to people getting started with crystals. In reading this book, I discovered that crystals carry energy within them, and all have different properties. I found out how important it is to cleanse all new crystals before you start using them (including jewelry), so you can remove any old energy they are carrying. It's also very powerful to set an intention for each crystal – What is that crystal's purpose? You can read all about different stones in that book. You better believe I was floored when I finally looked up what the properties of kyanite and fuchsite are!

Kyanite is excellent for meditation, stimulating intuition and helping spiritual energy to manifest into thought. Kyanite instantly aligns the chakras, clears the meridians, and restores energy to the physical body. It encourages speaking one's truth, cutting through fears and blockages. It opens the throat chakra and heals the thyroid. Whoa. Fuchsite channels information about treatments and holistic remedies, suggesting the most holistic action to take and receiving guidance on health matters and well-being. It also amplifies the energy of other crystals, releasing blockages and creating balance. In my situation at Deepak Chopra's center, the fuchsite inspired me to do the chakra healing, which is not something I had planned on doing. And it amplified the power of the kyanite, allowing me to heal my body and directly connect to my highest self. The insight and physical healing I received was truly remarkable!

So needless to say, I love meditating with crystals. I recently had a profound spiritual experience using amber, which I now wear daily. Amber is a powerful healer that draws disease from the body and aligns the chakras. It absorbs negative energy and transforms it into powerful positive energy that helps the body to heal itself. It provides protection while helping you to manifest your desires. It connects you to greater wisdom, promoting balance and patience, and develops trusting one's truth. Just what I need right now.

One thing I have discovered is that we are drawn to different stones and crystals at certain times in our lives, and they always carry the properties that we need at that particular moment. My best advice is to trust your intuition as you choose new crystals to use. If one stone feels better than the other, go with it, even if you think the other one is more beautiful. Go home, clean it by washing it and leaving it out in the direct sunlight or moonlight. Then bless your crystal, giving it a purpose and intention. Then start using it.

One beautiful daily practice I have is a gratitude rock meditation. I chose a beautiful fluorite palm stone to use as my gratitude rock. Every night before I go to bed, I hold this stone in my hand, close my eyes, and think of all the great things that happened to me that day that I'm grateful for. As I think of each thing, I imagine sending that positive, loving, gratitude energy into the stone in my hand. That crystal resides on my bedside table in a silk pouch. Now that I've been doing it for so long, all I have to do is touch that stone and I instantly feel the positive energy within it. Holding it makes me feel wonderful. What a beautiful gift to be able to access that positive energy anytime I need it. I hope this is a practice that you can enjoy too. These practices have the power to change your whole life. It's my intention to inspire you to get started and experience these positive shifts yourself.

Vanessa Cuccia - Chakrubs

One thing that I really want to get across to people is that crystals are not just inert mass -- they are sexy and should appeal to all sexual people! For a perspective on this, I decided to speak with Vanessa Cuccia, the creator and CEO of Chakrubs, The Original Crystal Sex Toy Company.

Vanessa told me her love of crystals began when she was a little girl and her family would crack open geodes they would find on the beaches of Long Island, New York. "As I grew older," she said, "I learned more about energy healing, and what crystals offer us regarding amplifying and cleansing our auric fields. I developed my concept and philosophy behind using crystals as a primary material for sex toys while I was an employee of a sex toy shop and living with a spirituality teacher."

I asked Vanessa what it was that inspired her to create a crystal sex toy. She told me that after years of working with Chakrubs, she discovered that this was part of her soul's path. "The crystals asked me to bring them to this light as part of the process for Divine Feminine Awakening," she said. "Many of my life experiences (if not all of them), were leading me to be the conduit for the crystals to do this sacred work. When I first had the idea, it was back in 2011 when I was living with a spiritual teacher and working at a sex toy shop. I had taken the job at the sex toy shop to put myself around knowledgeable, sex-positive people, who could help me understand my sexual hang-ups. I found myself being interested in their products. They carried everything: high-end vibrators, lingerie, books, you name it. But I realized at one point that I needed more than an orgasm. While pleasure was significant to me, I knew that along with my journey with sexuality, I had subconsciously learned to dissociate from my body. I needed to unlearn this; I needed to connect with myself. So, one night I went with my spiritual teacher friend to a woman's house, and she brought out a crystal-wand. Something 'clicked' within me, and I realized with a few adjustments it could be used as a sex toy. The name 'Chakrubs' entered my mind almost immediately, and my life changed. Crystals felt like a more intimate material to use than anything that was currently available at the store - silicone, stainless steel, wood, glass, squishy jelly-like substances. Crystals are beautiful, natural; they carry the history of the earth, as well as properties for well-being. I wanted this tool for my sexual and energetic healing, and I felt strongly that if I wanted it, others would, too."

Vanessa helped me to understand that working with a Chakrub helps the user connect to their self through what it represents. Not only is it crystal, which is already known for metaphysical healing, but it is created with the intention of empowering the user. When you purchase a Chakrub, you are making a decision, whether it's conscious or subconscious, to deepen your connection to yourself in the most intimate fashion, all while you experience pleasure. Because they are natural and beautiful, as well as unique (each Chakrub is different since it comes from the earth), it creates a mindset of pride in one's sexuality. Chakrubs have inspired lots of art and photographs from customers who see them as a symbol of self-love. The simple act of displaying it as a work of art instead of hiding it away in your sock drawer creates empowerment for the user and an overall deeper appreciation for one's sexual desires, removing shame from the equation. Since crystals are amplifiers and storage places of energy, adding the crystal element to our self-pleasuring sessions enhances the sensation of our sexual energy as well as that of the crystal.

Vanessa has new products constantly in development and is always striving to understand what her customers' needs are. She's also writing her own book "Crystal healing and sacred pleasure," about the methods she has developed harnessing the power of crystals for self-love, coming out in 2018.

Vanessa frequently receives page-long testimonials from her customers, bursting with excitement from what they experience with their Chakrubs. She asked me to share one of her favorite testimonials with my readers, which I'll reproduce below:

"My experience with this tool is a little different than most; I am a transgender male. At the time writing this, I am six months into hormone replacement therapy and admittedly still grasping to find my place in a society that demands that my anatomy is feminine, despite my identity. I struggle with this, it causes, at times, a great self-loathing which should not happen. I am comfortable with my physical self, yet am still pulled by societal expectations.

Months before I found Chakrubs, I was engaged in an intense spiritual experience where I found myself giving self-pleasure using an (unsafe, and not particularly ideal) amethyst pillar. My body jolted awake; it was beautiful, but not enough.

Somehow, I found my way to Chakrubs, where I lay eyes on the black onyx wand. I fell in love; I needed it. I dreamed about it; I felt everything in my mind and body pull me toward it.

I recently was able to purchase it, and in the short time we have been together it has completely bonded itself to my body, moving me effortlessly over its gorgeously smooth and cool length, absorbing my heat and sending it back to me, and soothing me to sleep at the end of my nights.

With it, I don't feel the self-conscious pressure that most other sexual objects caused me in the past. Instead, I feel my masculinity surging, my spirit opening and releasing that tension and allowing me to fall in love with the body I have, and tenderly wiping the sleep from my third eye all at once.

This is not a sex toy, or an object to be toyed with; these stones are metaphysical tools to be used to connect the physical self intensely to the spirit. Listen to your intuition and your body when you choose yours, allow yourself to fully open when you touch it to your skin, you will not regret it.

I am so thankful for this gorgeous opportunity to connect with myself, without feeling shameful of exploring my anatomy as a trans male. I feel powerful with this wand, and honestly it hasn't left my side since I got it in the post. Thank you so much."

Vanessa told me that since she started her brand in 2011, she has already seen powerful and positive shifts in the way our society is approaching sexuality and self-pleasure. There are many people in the industry dedicated to providing sexual education for those whom school fell short. The design and nature of Chakrubs are very welcoming to a wide range of people. The ethos behind the brand is rooted in self-realization, acceptance, and connection. Because of the metaphysical aspects of Chakrubs, the educational element is geared towards personal and spiritual growth. Vanessa's hope for Chakrubs is to create a sense of permission for people to explore their sexuality and spirituality. Her philosophy is that healing yourself will heal the world. The more love we can create, the better off we will be. But to understand love, we must understand ourselves in the most intimate of ways and beyond.

Most female-bodied people will use Chakrubs as a dildo, though she refrains from calling it a dildo, as the proper definition of that word means "artificial penis," whereas the original design of the Chakrub represents the sacred space within female bodies. They benefit from receiving pleasure from both the physical attributes of the stone as well as the metaphysical ones, creating intentional self-care practices through pleasure and mindfulness. Vanessa has created some products that are specifically for male-bodied people, and they would receive benefit in the same way.

Osahon Tongo, MFA - The Artist's View.

Next, I wanted to get an artist's perspective on crystal power. I decided to interview Osahon Tongo, a writer and producer originally from Naperville Illinois. Osahon was an athlete before he became known as a creative person. He went to Georgia Tech where he played D1 football for four years and won the ACC championship his senior year. Osahon pledged Omega Psi Phi during the 2008 season and he has been living as an example of manhood, scholarship, perseverance, and uplift ever since.

Osahon started in marketing just when social media started becoming a big thing. He developed as a social media specialist and was running digital marketing campaigns for big brands at the age of twenty-two. He then went to Greece to work at a Humane Society for a few months in 2011 as part of an AIESEC international leadership program. He was accepted into USC School of Cinematic Arts for writing and directing, and garnered many accolades including the Saks Scholarship for Mental Health Law Policy and Ethics, Annenberg Fellowship, Phi Kappa Phi, an Academy Award Nominated short film, work with James Franco on a feature film, and was a PD Soros Foundation for New Americans finalist. After he graduated he was selected for Ryan Murphy's inaugural diversity directing program. His short film "Iman and the Light Warriors" is premiering at HBO's ABFF.

As soon as I heard about these "light warriors" from Osahon I was intrigued. It sounded like the kind of mystical light that one can experience from crystals. I asked him about the Light Warriors project, and he told me, "The Light Warriors came to me after a deep meditation. I woke up and immediately started writing the scenes and the dialogue of the guardians of the light. It is of divine creation, so to speak. The original concept for the film was imagining Chiraq in a high concept world that brought destruction to inner city Chicago and explored how a young child could focus on love through all adversity. I think we all have that inner child that wants to express our emotions, love, and be loved. It takes extraordinary power to be that light in desperate times and that was why I decided they should be swagged-out super heroes. I say that, 'all my homies are superheroes on a quest to unlock our powers,' and I truly believe that. We are light warriors that are raising a collective consciousness to a higher frequency so that people can self-actualize and create peace on earth."

Clearly, crystals had inspired Osahon to great things artistically. Naturally I was curious to know how he had discovered the power that crystals held, and how he used them in his own life. Fortunately, he was happy to explain to me. "My brother collected rocks when we were growing up so I first played with crystals when I was five," he told me, "but I didn't know anything of the healing properties. I think I tried my first crystal in summer 2015. I was cruising in Malibu and I saw this amazing clear quartz arrowhead, and I felt an extreme strong weight when I put it on. I started reading about crystals and carrying them around -- and I can say that I think it was a huge shift in how I thought about everything around me. For me, I can feel crystals most when I sit quietly after I work out or when I'm in nature meditating. It's some real hippy shit, I know! But someone explained it to me pretty simply and I just enjoy it. Our bodies are super computers. We are all made of energy and there is an electric current running through our bodies. These crystals are conductors of energy and are found in computers. Therefore the same concept can be applied to us."

Osahon's story of discovering crystal was fascinating, and I wanted to know more about how he used crystals in his everyday life. He told me that he has an adventureine that he uses when he does "wild boy" sports. And, he said, "I use cleansing stones to clear my aura and clear energies. I usually try to find a crystal that can help cleanse me, one that can ground me, and one that can focus me or clear whatever my problem is. I meditate with crystals around me. I sometimes drink crystal water. Sometimes I don't carry crystals intentionally, but then I'll find some cyanite in my wallet. I think I'm that deep now that I'm finding lost crystals!"

Osahan is a great example of a person who is both very masculine and very artistic -- and who uses crystals to focus both of those energies that allow him to be the best version of himself that he can possibly be.

Healing Circles - Aravel Garduno

In order to find out more about healing circles I interviewed Aravel Garduno at Crystalline Goddess in

Los Angeles, CA. To start with, I asked her to tell her personal and professional story. As it turned out, I had asked the right question! "It's exactly how it sounds!" she responded. "It was a personal story that transposed into a professional life. That professional life evolved."

I wanted to know how it all happened. "It started when I was a little girl," she remembered, "with my excitement around shiny things. Whether they were rocks or whether they were crystals, I loved them and I was drawn to them. One day my father, who sold precious stones, asked if one of his children wanted to accompany him to Hong Kong for a buying trip. I was the oldest of eight siblings. I decided to go on a trip. He said that we would be traveling around the world and we would just stop in Hong Kong and then continue traveling to other cities around the world. During that trip is when the twinkle came into my eye. I discovered the tremendous excitement that jewels held for me. I loved handling them alongside my father. He bought them finished and I would price them. After the first trip, we went back another time. At that point, I was eleven years old, and as I got older that love of crystals stayed with me. During this time my father stressed my need of an adequate education. He hoped that I would get a college scholarship, so he suggested that I apply to the Air Force Academy. In the end, I was accepted in the Air Force Academy with a college scholarship, but I realized that my heart was not connected to the Air Force. Instead, it was connected to working with the gems, jewels, and crystals. After some deep thought about the matter, I chose to follow my heart and declined a $200,000 scholarship. This was not a decision to be taken lightly. Only two hundred people in the United States would receive such a scholarship each year. When I said no to that, it was the same as saying yes to what my heart was telling me I was meant to do."

What Aravel's heart knew she was meant to do, was to work with the preternatural powers of crystals. After she made the decision, she began to work in the jewelry business in Los Angeles, and then decided to work her way up as a specialist in the industry. She made enough money to pay for her specialized training at the Gemological Institute of America for her certification. Shortly after that she opened her own gem store. In that store, she sold mainly fine jewelry of precious gems and metals. That career lasted for approximately fifteen years, and she then expanded and opened a store in Beverly Hills.

Eventually she got to the point in her life where things had to have meaning -- and she couldn't find the joy and peace that she sought at her work with any regularity. She decided to connect with what her life truly needed, and to close her business in order to do just that. She completed the leases of the stores that she had outgrown. Then she took the jewelry and began to sell it at to private boutiques and art galleries as an in-house jewelry store designer, and frequently presented at trunk shows at many locations, including the boutique cruise lines Silver Seas and Crystal Cruise Lines. And finally, in about 2007, she let that all go to find the true essence of herself. She lived off the jewelry sales for a while. "While this was happening," she remembered, "I was healing on a continuous basis. During that healing and transformation, I began to see my true purpose and gifts: I am here in the world to offer these benefits and to show the way to others. This healing and spiritual unfolding is still happening."

Aravel's crystal experience is wide-ranging. While she began to work with the crystalline energetically about twelve years ago, it was about nine years ago that she started to work with the crystal skulls. The combination of both the crystalline and the crystal skulls provides a plethora of wisdom.

"I'm grateful that my journey started with the bling bling!" she laughed. "My childhood love of the sparkle of gems has moved me into working with the most powerful conscious energy."

Currently, she hosts healing circles in Los Angeles and online. Aravel is the only healer that I am aware of who facilitates powerful healings by combining work with the Goddess, Crystalline lineages, and Crystals.

Sammy - Crystals and Professional Success

For another look at how crystals have touched a person's life, I spoke with Sammy, a real estate broker/developer who lives in the Bayview neighborhood of San Francisco. He has recently discovered the power of crystals by first being attracted to their beauty!

I asked Sammy what words would be best to describe the effects that crystals could have, and the answer was simple: "CALMING, CENTERING, HEALING! They give me great perspective, the same feeling I get when I look into the stars! I feel I am a speck in the big picture!"

That's a feeling that countless crystal users can relate to, and it's one that I have no doubt that just as many non-users of crystals will want to achieve. I asked Sammy what advice might be useful for a person who was just getting into using crystals, and I think the advice will be helpful: "Don't over-think! Go with your gut feeling when buying and building your connections! Crystals are very powerful and they don't have judgement. They are not good, bad, right, or wrong. They just are!"

But like anything that is good for the soul and body, crystals have also been good for Sammy's professional life. "I recently had a couple that was struggling to sell their home and were getting very upset with each other and were caught in the 'Blame Game,' Sammy recounted. "I mentioned to them that they have to release this because it was blocking the sale of their home. I asked them to come to my office and meet me. I had brought in five of my largest crystals and had them sitting on the conference room table. While I was getting their coffee I noticed them touching the crystals and admiring them. When I returned they asked about them and I said I brought them for you. They said, 'What?' I said they are going to help you heal your relationship, and after a two-hour conversation and some tears, holding the crystals they found the power to forgive and love again! The house sold two days later!"

Rev. Gillian V Harris - Crystals' Healing Power

In order to get even more perspective, I decided to speak with Reverend Gillian V. Harris, an author, speaker, goal coach, and visualization specialist. "It's tricky for me to say when I discovered crystals," she told me, "because I came into this incarnation with a very strong but instinctive understanding about stones and crystals. I was very attracted to them. As a child,

I consciously started collecting them at about ten years old on trips across the desert when we'd stop at Indian reservation shops. Once I'd obtained a beautiful stone or crystal I was naturally drawn to keep and protect it. I knew that it was special and meant something but had no idea what!"

It wasn't until Gillian started practicing Reiki several decades later that she saw the power right before her eyes. Now, Gillian uses different stones and crystals to enhance an energy treatment: nephrite for emotional calm, rose quartz for emotional healing and compassionate self-forgiveness, rhodonite for confidence, selenite or amethyst to relieve stress and tension or to help feel more rested after a bad night, smokey quartz or auralite crystals to help relieve toxic emotions or negative caustic thoughts, amethyst or turquoise to release anxiety or fear. Her list is like an endless treasure trove of wisdom about how crystals can be used to improve our lives!

"For clearing people, places or things Selenite is amazing!" she advised. "It is my favorite energy disinfectant. Selenite is the bleach of the stones. Selenite naturally clears, constantly. So it stays cleared and it is excellent to use to clear other stones; to clear other people places and things!"

I wanted to know if Gillian had any interesting and inspiring stories that revealed the great mystical abilities of crystals. I was certainly not disappointed when I asked her! "One time," she recounted, "I had an associate who went missing for a couple days. She then called me forty-eight hours into her disappearance to tell me she'd tried to commit suicide by overdosing sleeping pills. For some reason she didn't die but instead was incredibly sick and now wanted to live! Her boyfriend (the one she says made her feel like killing herself!) took her to the hospital. A day later she called me. She was allowed a short phone call. She was on a psychiatric ward and her body was in trouble.

"After hanging up with her, I did a Distant Healing. In a Distant Healing, a Reiki Practitioner can perform healings from a distance. Any distance. There is no limit to life force energy which is what is being used when delivering Reiki. I visualized my friend and then put her on my healing table. I am generally guided by Spirit as to which stones to use. I placed them in specific places along the table where her different chakras would be. After spending some minutes doing work with light and Reiki symbols I wanted to scan her body using a wonderful twelve inch wand of Selenite that I held about twelve inches above the table. Starting from the head of the table I moved the wand down, slowly over her spirit body down to her toes. I was going to do this three times.

"I then moved the wand slowly from her feet back upward and as I passed the mid-torso area the wand snapped, with half of it falling to the table! It stunned me! I stopped in my tracks. Spirit absolutely had my attention. I got an immediate reading that there was so much toxicity in this area and that the selenite was working but that the toxicity had overpowered it. I was to understand that the selenite had done a great job drawing out a lot of the toxin but in doing that it was weakened to a fracture. I also got that I was to lay the other piece, still in my hand, down on the table next to the one that had fallen. I was to leave them there overnight and let them work on the spirit body of this young woman. The next day I talk to her again. She's doing much better. Her doctor says he's amazed that she's not in line for a liver transplant. He said that under normal conditions, after the number of pills she'd taken, a liver would have been irreparably damaged! Hers was going to be fine!"

Needless to say, that story stunned me! Gillian's ability to use crystal healing seemed nothing short of miraculous. And as always, I could not understand how anyone could fail to be interested in the incredible powers that they held. As Gillian explained to me, stones and crystals have served to amplify the non-physical reality of life. To merely marvel at them is to silently acknowledge the wonder which is outside the physical. Looking at a crystal makes you feel something. And it is a mystery beyond our human capacity for knowledge. How do they draw one to them as they do, and just how is it they make one want to touch them? Gillian explained, "I think what I'm trying to say is stones and crystals have illumined the reality of the multi-dimensionality of life. They themselves appear only physical – like humans. But then they radiate energy that actually effects change. Humans do that too! So, these beautiful rocks are alive -- just like us...just like everything! Stones and crystals have played into my much bigger view of all of life as one big living organism!"

Gillian is like an encyclopedia of crystal knowledge in some ways, but that doesn't mean that she doesn't know how to listen to her intuition and instinctive knowledge when it comes to understanding the crystal world. She explained to me, "I am stunned at how many stones I know now! Just from glancing I can probably identify a good fifty of them and can tell you the energetic qualities of about thirty of them! There are definitely some that I know the name but don't know exactly what they do. But here's the thing; when I need something -- confidence, emotional comfort, wisdom, physical stamina, or whatever it may be -- I know which stones to grab! I know which stones to meditate with or which to simply put in a bag and keep with me for the day. I got this by learning about these magical nuggets one at a time. I love to go to a metaphysical store that sells them and just let myself be drawn to whatever I'm drawn to. When I get home, I then learn about that particular stone! And remember, crystals are also communicators: A fun thing to do is to go into one of those stores with a question. Ask the question as you are allowing yourself to be guided to a stone! Remember which stone you chose in response to the question and look up the qualities of that stone later to get your answer!"

Gillian truly shows how familiarity with crystals exists at the crux of intuition and knowledge. As she put it, "I'd like it to convey the fact that crystals and stones are another tool given to us to help navigate through this incarnation! We can use them to enhance, calm or awaken energy. Use them to heal! Use them to empower a situation or intention! Use them to clear the air and to effectively clear a slate for a new beginning."

Gillian truly inspired me with her thirst for knowledge and her mastery over the powers that crystals wield. Truly she shows the great abilities and fulfillment that any of us can gain by opening ourselves up to a connection with crystals.

Raneika - Crystals and the Sober Life

Next, I interviewed Raneika about her crystal experience. Raneika is a forty-three-year old single mother of five children (twin boys age twenty-four, a seventeen-year old son, a fourteen-year old daughter, and a soon to be two-year old son). She works as a city planner with aspirations to begin law school in fall, 2018. Raneika told me she was introduced to the power of crystals by her mother when she was around twelve years old – although she didn't begin practicing and working with crystals on her own until she was thirty-seven years old.

Raneika told me that her beginning to work with crystals came as a result of her being recovered from drug and alcohol abuse and delving into spiritual development instead. She explained, "Being newly sober, I found myself in the process of recovery, which demanded the renewal of my mind and the nurturing of my spirit. Working with crystals started with my taking prayer and meditation classes at my spiritual center. Initially, crystals had a way of grounding me and connecting me to the earth. Over the last few years, my work with crystals has evolved to practicing with Yoni eggs while setting intentions for my life. Recently, my intuition guides me in which Yoni egg to insert and meditate with."

Raneika told me that crystals are, in her view, not just for those who are working to maintain a sober lifestyle, but for everyone. She told me, "The main piece of advice I'd offer for anyone just getting into crystals is to know that they're *always* guided to do what is true for them. I used to second-guess myself and my choices which only delayed my benefiting from the powerful healing energy available from crystals. Recently, I have my awareness of the power of different crystals in setting my intention for my use of crystals. The results are undeniable."

Raneika also gave me a list of some of her favorite crystals and what effects they have:

clear quartz – to amplify any intention I set for myself, heighten my intuition, overall cleansing and balancing chakras, sharper discernment.

rose quartz – compassion, love, empathy, tenderness

black obsidian – mental clarity, heightened intuition, clearing negative energy and confusion

carnelian – empowerment, courage, strength in my voice, sharpened intellect

I think those are qualities we are all looking for, no matter who we are! The moral, for Raneika, is this: "In general, I want people to feel empowered by the connection we have to all of creation. There's a certain confidence, relief, support, and empowerment in recognizing the many gifts of the planet that can be used as aids to assist us along the journey. As someone who struggled many years with the concept of God as a Divine Creative Intelligence, my use of crystals is one of the aids that has led to my spiritual awakening. I wish this to be true for others."

Crystals in England - Antonis

For yet another perspective on how crystals can enhance one's life, I decided to speak with Antonis who lives in England where he works in the financial services industry. Antonis told me he first discovered the power of crystals at the young age of only seven. Antonis was exposed to crystals for at least one month each year at the numerous Christmas markets of Germany. Next to traditional food, spiced sweets, and wooden toys, Christmas market stalls displayed small-to-medium-sized crystals every December. "There was something appealing about these crystals," he remembered. "I was not sure if it was the light, the cinnamon scent in Christmas markets, or the overall atmosphere that increased my fascination. The mineral that first caught my attention had a golden metal inclusion. Since I did not have enough pocket money with me on that day, I was not able to purchase that crystal. But I thought about it every night of that week until I was able to return the following Saturday to buy the crystal."

Since that day, crystals have continued to have a profound impact on Antonis in a way that is extremely personal to him. "The effects of crystals on us depend on who is feeling or observing the mineral," he explained. "For me it is fascinating to know that the mineral can be millions of years old, and to think about its origins as well as what part of the world it was found in. Who are the people that found the mineral and what might their story be? Remembering his own introduction to the crystal world, Antonis advised crystal newcomers to start small. "Try a German Christmas market for example," he counseled. "This will give you a feel for what's out there and will offer you a great variety in terms of crystals that you can touch and feel."

Everyone has their own individual way of interacting with crystals. And Antonis has done a fantastic job of finding his own way of interacting with them! "One of my means for examining new crystals was to smell them, next to touching and looking at them," he said. "At the age of nine there was a situation where a shopkeeper asked me what I was doing with the crystals, as he clearly observed me putting them one by one closer to my nose to smell them. It was a bit embarrassing as I was not the only client in the shop. I decided to leave the shop for the day and come back on a different day."

In short, as Antonis puts it, "Crystals are fascinating and I am not saying that everyone should own one or a collection of them, but everyone should make time to experience the effect of a crystal on them and their life."

Lupito - Crystal Singing Bowls

Crystals, of course, can take many forms. And to learn about one wonderful form that they can take, I decided to interview Lupito, the co-owner of Crystal Tones, about crystal singing bowls. I asked Lupito how he first became involved with crystals, and he told me that on August 18th of 1996, he had a spontaneous realization while he was awake. "My consciousness and understanding was accelerated during that time," he told me, "I had a new connection with the universe. I started to see colors more vividly and became more sensitive to light and sound. It was very challenging because I had such a rapid transformation, that people who knew me before, didn't understand me anymore; it was like I was speaking a different language. My heart was so full of love and inspiration, I wanted everyone to have this experience. Soon after that, I was out with my dog in my yard, sobbing, asking why this had happened to me.

I wanted to not be alone and to have people understand what I was going through. The universe said one clear message to me: 'crystal bowls.' After that, I knew they were my life's mission: to bring the consciousness and healing of the bowls to the world."

Needless to say, it sounds like a profound experience that anyone would want to have. But I wanted to know from Lupito more about how the bowls worked and what their history was. He filled me in on some background. "The classic frosted, the clear, and the ultra-light frosted crystal singing bowls were the first bowls we introduced at Crystal Tones," he recounted. "These series are made with pure quartz tuned to different notes, which correspond to different energy centers and meridians of the body. They were and are used for relaxation, meditation, and learning to be in the flow of life. They've also been used in group settings and by different kinds of therapeutic practitioners like sound healers and Feng Shui masters. The bowls in the past have generally been used in the same ways as now. But as time goes on, people are always innovating and integrating them with new practices. A relatively recent integration is how Yoga teachers play the bowls or have them played throughout their classes. Sound baths are also becoming more and more popular. A sound bath is where attendees lie or sit meditating, bathing in, and receiving the sounds of the bowls. The crystal bowls are also becoming more popular now in drug rehabilitation centers, for patients of cancer, in psychotherapy, and for weddings, childbirth, and funerals. The bowls are universal; they can be integrated with anything. You don't need to know anything about them to be able to benefit from them. Everyone uses them in their own way. Remember, the bowls *are* used for healing, but I like to remind everyone that the bowls are actually catalysts for us to open up to healing ourselves."

It's clearly an incredible range of uses that bowls have! I wondered, after Lupito's amazing experience, how the bowls had affected him in his own life. "Crystal singing bowls have enhanced my ability to see things for what they are," he explained. "Most of our lives we're subconsciously burying what isn't emotionally easy to deal with. This is an important lesson the bowls have taught me -- the importance of uncovering what we cover up in our minds. These cover-ups translate into subconscious limitations that dictate how we live. Learning this has made me a master of working with and liberating people on a profound level. The crystal bowls help me to do the work to liberate myself; they peel the layers of the onion."

But the personal benefits of the bowls have not just been internal. "What I have learned working with the bowls plays an important role in what I do with Crystal Tones," he told me. "The crystal bowls have brought me to many places, people, and cultures. These inspiring experiences have developed my abilities as a teacher. I've found the more I observe and see the subconscious programs people are running, the more I can clear my own and help others with theirs. The more we free ourselves from our blockages, the more we can enhance our abilities and strengths."

And for Lupito, while crystal bowls are wonderful in and of themselves, it is the human element that is truly most important. "The crystal singing bowls have attracted certain people into my life who love the bowls," he remembered. "I've found great friends and people who have been master teachers for me, people who have helped me move into the next stage of my evolution. For myself and Crystal Tones, this has made all of the difference in our success. A perfect example of this is when Paul Utz and I came together in the beginning of Crystal Tones. Paul served as an anchor for my visions. Together we were able to grow Crystal Tones over many years. We became business partners, traveled the country and eventually the world, taking the bowls everywhere. Paul and I brought together a worldwide family of distributors creating the foundation of Crystal Tones."

Lupito's story was, of course, very inspiring. I wanted to know from him how he goes about using crystal bowls to affect his customers. "The alchemy crystal singing bowls are the most profound tools I've ever used for transformation," he explained. "When I lecture, I always ask people to let me know if they have come across anything as profound as the bowls so that I can make it available to people using the bowls. In all of my travels and experience with Crystal Tones, we haven't found anything more profound. When making the bowls, we add gemstones, minerals, and metals to a pure quartz crystal base. The mixing of the different earth elements with the quartz enhances the bowl in a unique way where it changes the resonance and our ability to feel it. It gives the gemstone, mineral, or metal a song it could never sing before; this allows us to interact with them on a sonic level instead of just feeling their subtle energy. For the first time on the planet, the elemental kingdom was given a voice, a voice that vibrates from an organic, acoustic, crystalline instrument. All of the alchemical ingredients we mix with the bowls give a different essence or energy to them, giving us a different experience with them. It's like interacting with different personalities; each bowl is unique. Some of the bowls are relaxing and grounding while some are energizing, accelerating, and lift us up."

So how, I wanted to know, should the average person go about using these very powerful tools to help them in their own lives? "When people use the bowls on a daily basis, with intention, we see the best results," he counseled. "It doesn't matter what you practice, what modality you use; the bowls are about living from the heart and living with kindness. It is not uncommon for the bowls to be used and integrated in different cultures and organizations. This is one of the ways the bowls bring people of all kinds from all over the planet together."

And, he told me, one of their greatest benefits is one that the average user may not even expect: "One of the most positive effects of the bowls is that people learn to find their true self. They find their true essence allowing their life's purpose to become realized. And many times these people who have this realization start to share their experience by playing the bowls for others. From working with a small group of friends to traveling the world doing workshops and playing crystal bowl concerts, the bowls empower people to change their lives, then bring that same change to others."

"Another positive effect," he went on to explain, "is that the process of consciousness or psychological transformation is sped up by playing the bowls regularly.

They help us bring the subconscious to the conscious so we can take a look at our blockages, communicate and process them, and then release them. They help us create the space to do so where we normally would not have on our own. The bowls take you from a transformational pathway to a transformational highway. This becomes apparent in different ways such as changing bad habits and starting to take accountability for our lives. Taking accountability and accepting responsibility for all that we experience is key. We then start seeing how we create, indirectly or directly, everything we go through in life. And with this realization, we see how to create a new reality; we see how to manifest harmony and happiness. Clearing our mind of denial and thought viruses enables us to 'lighten our load', to be more free and liberated in life so we can move into new unprecedented possibilities of the future."

He summed up the user experience of crystal bowls this way: "When using the bowls we start to see the reflection of our soul, we see our true self to the degree that it merges with body, mind, and spirit. This awakens our creativity, sense of well-being, and balance. Simultaneously, we find a sense of home within ourselves that is normally left unfound. It gives us a feeling of completeness and knowing that relieves anxiety and satisfies. This helps unlock our connection to the universe, bringing forth our special abilities. It moves us into the rhythm and flow, the joy, the dance of life."

As I imagine anyone would be, I was stunned by the great powers and huge possibilities of the crystal bowls he described. I wanted to know more about the specific products. "We have over a hundred different alchemies and designs available and yet they are all unique," he explained to me. "They all work with different aspects of self. It can be intimidating for a newcomer to know where to start. What's most important in choosing bowls is the alchemy; this is more important than any other attribute. The best way to decide on which alchemies for your first bowls is to look at areas of your life that you'd like enhanced. Then, either match that up with a specific alchemy, consult with us, or any bowl master to recommend which bowls would work best."

But how could the average person choose the best bowl for themselves? "The ideal bowls for you are the ones that address the parts of yourself or your life that you wish to work on," Lupito advised. "Here are a few examples: if you're dealing with excess stress, sadness, or anger, we may recommend alchemies like charcoal, smoky quartz, laughing Buddha, or black tourmaline because they help us integrate centeredness, calmness, and joy. For somebody who is insecure, feels they lack support, or wants more love and nurturing in their relationships, we might recommend rose quartz, mother of platinum, rhodochrosite, morganite, or emerald. Or, for boosting creativity, thinking outside of the box, and being in the flow: ocean gold, moldavite, labradorite, and diamond activate those energies. You can see that by getting a combination of say three, five or twelve different bowls you can have a set that works on the whole body, mind, and spirit. This is why we recommend getting sets of different alchemy combinations. We also always tune the different notes of the bowls together to make the set have a song no matter how or who plays them. A harmonically tuned set is just as important as the alchemies within it. The bowls work like different medicines for different ailments; first is the diagnosis and second is the prescription. We customize each set for the individual and for how or where they will be using them. We personalize them. To us, it is not sales -- it's being in service."

Lupito's expertise deeply impressed me. I wanted to know what some of his most popular products were, and what impressed people about them. "The most popular alchemy bowls relate to the most basic traits of what it means to be human," he answered. "Laughing Buddha, aqua aura gold, and rose quartz are a few. Laughing Buddha, which is made with iron, helps us laugh more, be in the joy, and remember to not be so serious all the time. Aqua aura gold because it opens us up; it expands our intuitive abilities and enhances creativity. Rose quartz for its heart centeredness and love-activating qualities. While this may generally be the case, at the same time, it's hard to say what is most popular because it depends on the person and what speaks to them; it depends on where the person is in their life's journey."

I was truly overwhelmed by the knowledge and experience that Lupito showed. So lastly, I couldn't help wondering just where he gained all this incredible expertise. "My relationship with nature and the crystal and mineral kingdoms started as a child," Lupito recalled. "I've learned their properties through experience and over time. My highly creative and intuitive mind has helped me make this connection. The universe always highlights the information for me. This is done in a very childlike and playful way where you have to be paying attention to many dimensions all at the same time to see it. You could say it is an organic or indigenous style of learning. The characteristics of minerals, crystals, and metals mirror the human soul; you will see this by observing cultures and people and how they function. Then, by interacting and practicing feeling the subtle energies of the minerals, crystals, and metals, you can link the two worlds together. This is a self-teaching process where you must connect with all the layers of your environment and 'INvironment.' The different ingredients of the alchemy bowls represent the different dimensions of human nature, but they're also tools to bring harmony and balance into these areas of our lives."

That's a harmony and balance that I am sure we all want to achieve, and I know that Lupito's story will help at least some of us achieve it.

Eduardo F. Nieto- Crystals to the Power of 1

My next interview on the powers of crystals was with Eduardo F. Nieto of Sacred Space," the all-around designer." I wanted to see how crystals could help improve the life of someone who uses his creativity visually -- and Eduardo fit the bill perfectly with his wide range of design endeavors.

Eduardo designs in the categories of architecture, industrial and decorative products, environmental interiors, graphics (focusing on branding), and last but not least, event production. Event production is where Eduardo feels he can most artistically express himself. "An event is like a painting," he told me. "The venue is your canvas, the subject is your theme, and you color it with people just like in a painting. You select the hues to accommodate the subject. In an event your most important ingredient is the people, and how you guide them to participate in the theme is the art form."

This speaks to Eduardo's general theory of artistic design. "All design disciplines are basically the same," he believes. "This is due to the two main attributes -- creativity coupled with knowledge, the understanding of the techniques that are applied to each discipline. In other words you must have the education and the nomenclature for each of the fields that you are designing in."

Eduardo told me that his introduction to crystals was from a profound event in his life. "Nicole, my soul mate and wife, contracted breast cancer," he remembered. "This event gave us a reality check. It made us look inward into the causes of such a devastating turn of events. This event guided Nicole on a path of discovery not only for her cure but for her reason for existence. Her path to recovery was abrupt, from her eating habits to every other aspect of her life. The decisions that she made were amazing: Yoga (she became an instructor), art, music (she amplified her voice talent to the degree that she was booked at the Paris Hotel in Las Vegas), meditation, (she studied it, practiced it, and taught it) and spirituality, (she was exposed to the power of crystals and how to use a crystal pendulum for guidance."

"Her malady affected me in profound ways," he confided, "as I observed her tenacity and desire for a healthy discipline in her life. I was a benefactor too, as I began to change my point of view on physical, mental, and spiritual health and how to preserve it. She was my teacher, and she opened my eyes, heart and mind in many ways. What has really given me the edge at being a designer is the knowledge of crystals and how they work. Crystals are not static. They have a life of their own. They morph from one platonic plan to another. They follow the principles of Sacred Geometry. With this information, I immersed myself in the subject of sacred geometry, and on that path I became profoundly aware of how the Universe works and thus found ancient secrets that I could apply -- especially in the subject of crystals. I developed my personal connection with the Almighty through the use of my crystal pendulum. I was able to surrender myself to the divine information that comes to me, which helps my personal and intellectual views -- especially in design. I believe that we live in a factual universe that is connected to all things. Therefore, with my pendulum I am able to tap into universal knowledge. It is my communication tool to all things. The reality is that my pendulum is my higher self, and is just a gauge on the dash board for me to read."

Eduardo places great stock not just in crystals, but especially in the crystal pendulum. And he particularly recommends them to those who are just beginning their crystal journey. "Find your personal pendulum," he advises. "Or better yet -- let it find you. There are crystal practitioners who have charged crystals. A crystal is a warehouse for knowledge of the spirit, and like anything else each crystal needs exposure to other, all-knowing, crystals. So, if a crystal is in the proximity of another crystal with information, it charges itself to have the same energy. There is an ancient relic called MAX the Crystal Skull. MAX has a wonderful history, look it up."

Here Eduardo provided me with a URL where we could find more information about MAX: http://www.crystalskulls.com/max-crystal-skull.html

"The point is," he said, "MAX has many little brothers and sisters, crystals that have been placed in the same room with MAX to be charged. When a crystal is charged other crystals near it automatically have shared the same energy and information. The charging process of crystals is like wireless charging of a battery. In other words, MAX has lineage. Go to Aravel Garduno's website for charged crystals," he said. I smiled, knowing that Eduardo was recognizing the wisdom of one of my other favorite interview subjects!

"Get a dowser (the traditional name for a pendulum)," he advised. "Aravel or any other crystal practitioner will show you how to use it. You will be pleasantly surprised how it will respond to you. Get in tune with your dowser and have it with you all the time and when in doubt ask your higher self through your dowser."

Finally, "Crystals," Eduardo concluded, "are for everyone with an open mind and a sense of adventure. Given the information, those seeking enlightenment and a rollercoaster, mind-thrilling ride will try my recommendations." I couldn't agree with him more!

Science

As yet, little is known to science about just how crystals do their incredible work. One popular theory is called "the placebo effect." It holds that crystals can work their healing miracles only because the user believes in their power, and this has a beneficial effect on the body.

But there are other scientific ways in which the power of crystals could be explained. Some say that science is familiar with the many uses of crystals in the world of Western medicine—but most may not be aware of it. Some crystals may contain trace amounts of healing materials. Kunzite is a gem that many crystal users employ for an uplifting feeling, and it contains lithium, a drug that doctors use to treat depression. Malachite contains copper, which can be used to treat arthritis, but it is through the medium of the crystal that we are affected. Obviously, eating pennies would not have the same benefits! The crystal is a special material that allows the copper to do its work. Still, many people who actually use crystals say that they feel the effects from that simple contact with known minerals, which science can't explain. Can science tell us anything about this spiritual element? So far, Western academics have told us nothing about the spiritual element of crystals' power.

Put simply, a person may feel better after undergoing a crystal healing treatment, but there is no scientific proof that this result has anything to do with the crystals being used during the treatment. In 2001, Christopher French and his colleagues at Goldsmiths College at the University of London, presented a paper at the British Psychological Society Centenary Annual Conference in Glasgow, in which they outlined their study on the efficacy of crystal healing.

For the study, eighty participants were asked to meditate for five minutes while holding either a real quartz crystal or a fake crystal that they believed was real. Before meditating, half of the participants were primed to notice any effects that the crystals might have on them, like tingling in the body or warmth in the hand holding the crystal.

After meditating, participants answered questions about whether they felt any effects from the crystal-healing session. The researchers found that the effects reported by those who held fake crystals while meditating were no different from the effects reported by those who held real crystals during the study.

Many participants in both groups reported feeling a warm sensation in the hand holding the crystal or fake crystal, as well as an increased feeling of overall well-being. Those who had been primed to feel these effects reported stronger effects than those who had not been primed. However, the strength of these effects did not correlate with whether the person in question was holding a real crystal or a fake one. Those who believed in the power of crystals (as measured by a questionnaire) were twice as likely as non-believers to report feeling effects from the crystal.

"There is no evidence that crystal healing works over and above a placebo effect," French told Live Science. "That is the appropriate standard to judge any form of treatment. But whether or not you judge crystal healing, or any other form of [complementary and alternative medicine], to be totally worthless depends upon your attitude to placebo effects."

As French pointed out, there are many forms of treatment that are known to have no therapeutic effect other than a placebo effect. However, while these treatments might make you feel better temporarily, there is no proof that they can actually cure diseases or treat health conditions. "If you're suffering from a serious medical issue, you should seek treatment from a licensed physician, not an alternative healer," French said

My ideas for a new case study might look like this: One idea would be the use of an electromagnetic machine like a Quantum Magnetic Resonance Analyzer with two groups of people. One group will purchase crystals in hopes of healing their situation, and the other group will not purchase crystals. A member would be instructed not to tell the examiner which group each member belongs to at the time of the examination. After a couple of weeks of having the crystal with them every day, or not having them, each member would be retested for a symptom to see if their body's energy has, in fact, corrected itself. The other idea for a new case study might look like this: use of an electromagnetic machine with two groups of people, one group with fake crystals and the other group with real crystals. The examiner would not only identify with each participate group member by their questionnaire results but also the frequency levels in the real crystals and the fake crystals.

I can only hope that science will continue its search for understanding of exactly how crystals work to increase our bodies' healing energies!

Crystals and Authenticity

Since I started work on this book, I have had an eye-opening experience that I feel I need to share with my readers. Not long ago, I went to a crystal store because I heard they had amazing deals.

The store had upbeat disco music playing, and of course had lots of crystals. Speaking with Aravel has helped me to know the difference between high-and low-quality crystals, since she is a jeweler. As a result, I could tell that a lot of the merchandise in this store was low grade and fake.

But it made me realize that a person new to crystals and without my experience might not realize that they were fake, and they could easily be taken in. It's important that you ask critical questions, and use your intuition on what is real or not real when you buy crystals.

Ask the shopkeeper what grade crystals they sell and why. From where do these crystals originate? How does the distributor inspect the crystals to make sure they are real? How can we tell if these are natural or man-made, unnatural crystals? If the location lets you know that your crystals are man-made or mixed with a majority of additional materials like glass, plastic, or other items, you may not want to buy from that store.

But before you go shopping, you must know if your crystal is real or fake. I interviewed Dan a representative of the International Gemological Institute to find out more about this. "The only way to determine if a crystal is real is to take it to a laboratory and have it graded," he told me. "Gems are graded based on clarity and treatment. The clearer and more natural, the better the grade of that gem. An example of that would be with an emerald. You can take an emerald to a certified laboratory like Gemological Institute of America or International Gemological Institute to find out if it is natural, or has been heat-treated."

In fact, Dan told me, some gems have been treated with heat, oil, and other material that makes the inclusions less visible. "There are all types of shapes of crystals," he explained. "Gems come out of the ground and look like rocks without polish and luster. These gems go to a gem cutter to facet and polish the stones, and that gives them the look that you see in your local jewelry store. The treatment of the gems depends on the stone and the need for a particular look. All of this information will be provided to you once you take it to be tested to find out if it is real or fake."

As always, when dealing with crystals and gemstones, your intuition is your best friend. If you get bad vibes from a store or a gemstone, stay away!

Nellie Barnett - Science, Crystals, and the GIA

To get you more information about crystals in science, I got in touch with Nellie Barnett, the Public and Media Relations Manager for GIA, the Gemological Institute of America. She coordinated with GIA's Richard T. Liddicoat Gemological Library and Information Center to provide me with some fascinating information.

First, she provided the Institute's official definitions, showing the distinction between crystals and gems:

A crystal is defined as a mineral with a regular internal arrangement of atoms producing flat surfaces that have definite angular relationships. The crystal shape is an external expression of both the internal structure and the strength of the chemical bonding in the structure.

A gem variety is subcategory of gem mineral species. A variety can be based on color, transparency, or phenomenon. Gems must be beautiful, durable and rare.

It's important to bear these distinctions in mind. Though, of course, both crystals and gems can have similarly mystical energy powers! "Rose quartz and amethyst are both varieties of the mineral quartz, which is silicon dioxide (SiO_2)," Nellie told me. "Quartz is a common mineral on earth, however, most quartz is not gem quality. Only when it possesses sufficient transparency and color saturation is it faceted or polished and used as a gem. Most minerals can form as crystals. However, most minerals do not have a gem variety."

I wanted to make sure that the GIA was a good place for testing the authenticity of gems and crystals after my eye-opening experience at the one shop. And to my relief, Nellie answered that "GIA tests every material submitted to determine whether it is natural or not, and discloses any treatments discovered during our examination."

For those interested in testing a piece, she explained, "There are three ways to submit a gemstone to GIA. The first is to submit your gemstone through your local jeweler. The second is to ship your gemstone directly to one of our laboratories. The third way is to bring your gemstone to any of sixteen drop-off locations in eleven countries. Visit https://www.gia.edu/gem-lab for more information."

Finally, I asked Nellie about what certain scientists had said about gems containing copper or lithium. "Some gems and minerals contain one or more trace elements," she explained, "which are atoms that aren't part of the mineral's essential chemistry. Some trace elements can influence a gem's color or crystal shape. To determine the trace-element chemistry of a gem material, it would need to be tested." So, it seems the scientific jury is truly still out on what exactly causes the magnificent effects that we observe in crystals and gems!

Hopes and Dreams

My dream is to have the United States of America one day valuing the use of Eastern-medicine healing in addition to Western medicine. I feel this balance of the two can increase the current imbalance and lack of success with the healing of our people. I believe that when we activate this balance, the human race will be able to heal not just themselves but, the world's illness in a powerful way. I hope that the current government, medical and pharma industries work in support of these items focusing away from profit, but instead focusing towards benefiting not only this generation but also future generations.

I hope that this book has shown you clearly the vast effect that crystals can have on the lives of all kinds of people, in big and small ways. I think crystals are reaching a turning point in their popularity. And you can be a part of that turning point. No one book can ever tell you all that you need to know about crystals. As the many testimonials in this book say, the only way truly to discover what secrets crystals hold for you is to go to a crystal store and discover them for yourself. My wish is that someday, when you have amassed a wonderful collection of crystals that fill your life with joy, peace, and healing energy, you will think back to this book, and fondly remember how it brought the first sliver of the light and deep knowledge of the world of crystals into your life. May you become the amazing Buddha who holds the precious gems that inspire you to be the superhero that you dream of being forever.

Congratulations after reading this book you are officially a Superhero Buddha. Namaste!

Printed in the United States
By Bookmasters